Northern Territories Travel Guide

Sightseeing, Hotel, Restaurant & Shopping Highlights

Jack Woods

Table of Contents

Northern Territories

The Northern Territories are known as the 'real outback' of Australia and it depicts nature on a large, impressive scale. The state contains some of the most famous natural attractions in Australia and is bounded by Western Australia, Queensland and South Australia. The major city is Darwin, Australia's gateway to the Far East and to the sparsely populated Outback. It is a city characterized by the vibrant fusion of east and west.

Darwin enjoys beautiful waterfront scenery, thanks to its location along the Timor Sea, while the landscape makes way for timeless desert, monsoon forests and mysterious geographic formations, as you head south towards the heart of Australia.

Sites such as Ayers Rock, known also known by its Aboriginal name of Uluru and the Kakadu National Park combine natural splendour with mystical significance.

Gaze at rock paintings that date back thousands of years or connect with the spirit of the land, through an intimate encounter with the Aboriginal culture.

The wildlife of Australia is different from in the other continents. It is home to the kangaroo and the wallaby and the emu, as well as a colorful variety of birdlife and some of the meanest crocodiles to be found anywhere. Crocosaurus Cove offers the rare adrenaline rush of a safe swim with these ancient behemoths. For a unique accommodation option, consider Feathers Sanctuary, a bed and breakfast located within a private bird park. (http://www.audleytravel.com/destinations/australasia /australia/accommodation/feathers-sanctuary.aspx)

Fans of aviation history may find the whole Northern Territory fascinating, as pioneering aviators feature prominently in the region's history. Darwin was, for instance, the only part of Australia that was extensively bombed by the Japanese during World War Two. Both Darwin and Alice Springs have museums dedicated to the history of aviation and Katherine, 300km south of Darwin, also has a few flying legends in its general museum. Equally fascinating, is the story of Australia's unlikely pioneers of long distance travel - the cameleers from Afghanistan.

Expect the unexpected, from this northern tip of the Deep South and be sure to pack a good camera to remember all your adventures in this scenic land.

Culture

Australia has a predominantly Western culture which is strongly influenced by its colonization by Britain. English is the language used by most of its inhabitants and English sport, such as rugby and cricket are also very popular. 68 percent of the Northern Territory's population is European with most hailing from England, Ireland and Scotland.

In Darwin, however, the influence of the Asia is a noticeable factor. Australia has a large Chinese community, which includes people from Mainland China, Hong Kong, Timor and Taiwan. In Australia, facilities such as temples are often shared by different faiths, such as Buddhism and Taoism. The Chinese represent about 4 percent of the Northern Territory's people.

Besides Chinese, Indonesia also exerts some cultural influence on Australia. Indigenous people of Australia have had trade relations with Makassans from Indonesia from the mid 1600s and their trade fostered relationships between different Aboriginal groupings and even gave them a shared language in the form of pidgen Makassan. During the mid to late 19th century, Indonesian workers were brought to Australia and, following Japan's occupation of former Dutch colonies during World War Two, Australia, along with Britain played a role in ousting the Japanese. Today, Indonesian is taught as a non-compulsory second language in Australian schools and the cuisine makes a popular alternative to Chinese and Thai food.

About 40 percent of the Northern Territory is held by Aboriginal land trusts and tribes representing over 40 different language groups are spread throughout the area. They represent one of the world's most ancient living cultures. The concept of Dream Time forms an integral part of the spirituality and social code of all Aboriginal groupings. Tribes are divided into smaller family clans, each of which have their own collection of symbols and sacred sites. Dream Time reflects into the everyday doings of people. It also refers to a dynamic and mythic past when giant super beings roamed the earth, and leaving their imprint on it, through their adventures. The largest Aboriginal communities in the Northern Territory are the Pitjantjatjara near Uluru, the Arrernte around Alice Springs, the Luritja, the Warlpiri and the Yolngu around Arnhem land.

Visitors should bear in mind that a number of alcohol restrictions exists in parts of the Northern Territory. In Alice Springs, Katherine and Tennant Creek alcohol for private use cannot be bought before 2pm and it may not be consumed within 2km of a licensed venue or within remote Aboriginal communities. Restrictions also apply in some sections of Darwin.

Location & Orientation

The Northern Territories lie along the Timor Sea, 656km from Dili, the capital of East Timor, 1,818km from Port Moresby in Papua New Guinea and 2,700km from Jakarta, the capital of Indonesia.

There are regular flights from Singapore to Darwin and Darwin is also connected by air to various major Australian cities such as Sydney, Perth and Adelaide. A single highway, Stuart Highway, connects Darwin by road to Alice Springs and Adelaide. From Tennant Creek, Barkly Highway connects the Northern Territory to Queensland and from Katherine, Victoria connects to Western Australia. As travel through the Northern Territory involves long distances, travel by rented car or through tour operators may be the best way to cover as much of the region's attractions as possible.

There is also a tourist train, The Ghan (http://www.greatsouthernrail.com.au/site/the_ghan.jsp), which connects Darwin to Adelaide, via twice weekly trips, with stops at Katherine, Tennant Creek and Alice Springs. The service has been operational for more than eighty years. Bear in mind, this is a scenic excursion, with the train making a five hour stop in Katherine and a four hour stop in Alice Springs along the way. The travel time runs approximately between 51 and 54 hours.

One of Darwin's most affluent suburbs is the coastal neighbourhood of Larrakeya, which includes the Myilly Point Heritage district, as well as the botanical gardens and the popular Mindil Beach area. Other suburbs are Brinkin, Coconut Grove, Millner and Karama.

Climate & When to Visit

Darwin's weather is characterized by two main seasons of wet and dry weather. The wet season falls in the summer months, which is from December to March, when spells of intense rainfall and periodic storms occur. Floods and cyclones are not unusual during this time, and many attractions are closed or inaccessible due to flooding risk.

The rain provides a slightly moderating effect on temperatures, but day temperatures can still average around 32 degrees Celsius with night temperatures typically staying around 25 degrees Celsius. November tends to be the hottest month around Darwin, as it is just before the rainy season begins and day temperatures of around 34 degrees Celsius are usual. Even in the winter months from June to August, day averages still tend around 31 degrees Celsius, but night temperatures drop to between 19 and 20 degrees Celsius. The autumn months are pleasant and dry. One of the most popular months for tourists is September.

Towards the south, the Northern Territory progressively becomes drier and extreme temperatures can be experienced. For example, at Uluru/Ayers Rock, summer temperatures can go as high 47 degrees Celsius in summer or as low as -7 degrees Celsius in winter. Kakadu National Park experiences a six season cycle. Yegge, from May to June is cool and misty. Wurrgeng, from June to August, is cold and relatively dry. In mid-August, this gives way to Gurrung, a hot, dry spell that lasts till October.

From mid-October through to December, humidity builds as the monsoon period becomes eminent. This is known as Gunumeleng. Gudjewg, from January to March is when the monsoon breaks with heavy rains, thunderstorms and flooding. In April, comes Banggereng and the rain clears, although occasional wind storms still occur.

Sightseeing Highlights

Darwin

Darwin is the largest city in the Northern Territory and also its capital. Its convenient proximity to Southeast Asia has made a gateway to the East. The city has no direct connection to the famous Charles Darwin, but was named after him by one of his former shipmates from his voyage aboard the Beagle.

If you wish to take in the city's beautiful seaside location, stroll along the Darwin Wharf Precinct. On a hot day, you can enjoy a cooling splash or two in the wave pool, which offers swimming safe from Australia's fearsome sea crocodiles. There is a toddler pool and sunbeds, umbrellas, body boards and inflatable rings are available. Admission to this attraction is A$7. You can also relax on a bench, on the grass or seated at one of the area's cafes or restaurants. Fancy a movie? Take a seat at the Deckchair Cinema (http://www.deckchaircinema.com.au/), an open air theatre located in a tropical garden. It offers beautiful sunset sea views, before you settle down for the film show, which could feature innovative independent festival movies or classics from yesteryear.

There are two marine attractions. Indo Pacific Marine, on the Stokes Hill Wharf, seeks to educate visitors about the biodiversity of coral reefs. At Aquascene (http://aquascene.com.au/on Doctors Gully road, you can experience the rewarding thrill of hand feeding a variety of fish, including butterfly fish, batfish; milkfish, bream, catfish, parrot fish, diamond fish and cod. Admission is A$15.

A somewhat austere historical facility is the Fannie Bay gaol, located along East Point Road, where visitors can view the gallows and the wire enclosed cells, with blocks for males, females and children, as well as two isolated garden cells for the mentally ill. The prison was in use from 1883 to 1979.

The Museum & Art Gallery of the Northern Territory at Conacher Street on Bullocky Point, you can view a mixed palette of Darwin's natural and man made heritage. There is a large variety of Aboriginal art and the remains of a good selection of indigenous fauna. A prize specimen is the body of Sweetheart, a 5.1m seawater crocodile that had been the scourge of boats and other vessels during the mid to late 1970s.

There is also an exhibition and video clips to illustrate the devastation wreaked by Cyclone Tracy in 1974. High rollers can try their luck at the Skycity Darwin Casino, while speed junkies can test their skills at racing and drifting at the Hidden Valley Motor Sports Complex.

Apart from its own charms, Darwin offers a great base from which to explore other attractions of the Northern Territory, such as Alice Springs, Ayers Rock or Uluru (as it is now known), Kakadu National Park and the Tiwi Islands, where Aboriginal culture merges with Polynesian influences.

Crocosaurus Cove

Corner of Mitchell & Peel Streets,
Darwin, Northern Territory, Australia
Tel: 61 8 8981 7522
http://www.crocosauruscove.com/

Crocodiles are common in Australia and they feature prominently in legends, popular culture and aboriginal folklore. Their size, appearance and aggression make them seem formidable and dangerous, but in reality, a surprisingly small number of people are harmed crocodiles each year.

You can meet and greet over 70 different reptile species in the reptile enclosure at Crocosaurus Cove, including bearded dragons and snakes. At the turtle sanctuary, you will be able to view a variety of Australian freshwater species, including snapping turtles, red and yellow-faced turtles and pig nosed turtles. As far as the crocodiles go, you will be able to handle a hatchling, assist with feeding juveniles and view a powerful demonstration of the bite force of a fully grown adult.

For adrenaline junkies, the highlight will be a 15 minute session inside the Cage of Death. In this immersive activity, visitors are lowered in a transparent cylindrical cage, to share a crocodile enclosure with its owners, enjoying 360 degree views from up close and personal. Booking may be necessary to avoid disappointment. Another unique experience will be swimming with crocodiles. Professional glossy photographs will be taken of some of the activities and are available for sale. Admission is A$32, but some activities are charged separately.

Other Crocodile Farms

There are other facilities for crocodile watching. The Darwin Crocodile farm (http://www.crocfarm.com.au/) has a population of up to 10,000 crocs and you can enquire about holiday work, if your visa allows it.

There are informative displays to illustrate the life cycle of the crocodile. Crocodylus Park (http://www.crocodyluspark.com.au/) at 815 McMillans Road, Knuckey Lagoon is a small zoo that also houses lions, tigers, emus, kangaroo, wallaby, iguanas, pythons, anacondas, various types of monkeys and turtles. The crocodiles are the main attraction and the park has several species. There is a crocodile museum, a viewing platform for feeding times and a gift shop selling crocodile related merchandize. You will also have the opportunity to handle baby crocodiles. Admission is A$40. Tours happen at 10am, 12pm and 2pm.

Defence of Darwin Experience

5434 Alec Fong Lim Drive
East Point, Darwin,
Northern Territory 0801, Australia
Tel: 08 8981 9702
http://www.defenceofdarwin.nt.gov.au/

Fans of military history will probably love a visit to the
Defence of Darwin Experience, a museum that focuses on
Darwin's role in World War Two. It is a little known fact
that Darwin had been more heavily bombed than Pearl
Harbour. This event is graphically depicted in a series of
informative and interactive displays that highlight the
events of 19 February 1942.

Video footage features interviews with servicemen based
in the North Territory and also documents the war
experience from the perspective of different individuals.
An outdoor exhibition introduces visitors to the massive
guns, tanks, cannons and other assorted military vehicles.
Admission is A$14. There is a small gift shop, as well as a
cafe that serves snacks.

Australian Aviation Heritage Centre

557 Stuart Highway Winnellie,
Darwin, Northern Territory 0821, Australia
Tel: 8 8947 2145
http://www.darwinsairwar.com.au/

Anyone with even a passing interest in aviation, would be
well advised to pay a visit to the Australian Aviation
Heritage Centre. Darwin's air facilities played a key role
in both civilian and military aviation and some of the
legends to pass over Darwin include Amelia Earhart,
Amy Johnson, Bert Hinkler and Kingsford Smith, the
Australian who made the first trans-Pacific flight. The star
exhibit is a huge B52 bomber, on permanent loan from the
United States Air Force. Other planes from different eras
include a Sabre jet, a mirage, a spitfire and a tiger moth.
There are also historical photographs, audio-visual
material detailing the Japanese raid of 19 February 1942
and other memorabilia. The gift shop sells books and
related souvenirs. Admission is A$14.

Chinese Temple & Museum Chung Wah

25 Woods Street,
Darwin, Northern Territory 0800, Australia
http://www.chungwahnt.asn.au/

The Northern Territory has a large and fairly diverse Chinese community, dating back to the 1870s and it includes people of Hong Kong, mainland China, Timor and Taiwan. The first Chinese temple was built in 1887 and its current temple was built in 1977, following the damage to the previous one by World War Two and Cyclone Tracy. It follows a busy calendar of festivals, since the facility is shared by Buddhists, Taoists and followers of Confucius.

The entrance is guarded by stone lions crafted in China and a sacred Bodhi tree, said to be a descendant of the one under which Buddha sat when he attained enlightenment, grows on the grounds. The museum is manned by volunteers and has limited hours. Do act respectfully when visiting the temple. Do not touch any of the objects on the altar and avoid photographing visitors.

Pudakul Aboriginal Cultural Tours

Arnhem Highway, Adelaide River,
Darwin, Northern Territory, Australia
Tel: 61 0 8984 9282
http://www.pudakul.com.au/

The Pudakul Aboriginal Cultural experience introduces
visitors to a wealth of information regarding wildlife,
native plants, spirituality and aboriginal family life. There
are demonstrations to educate about indigenous weaving
techniques, spear throwing, clay sticks and playing the
didgeridoo. Local food and bush medicine is also covered
in the presentation. There are daily two hour tours
starting at 10.30am from April through to November. The
cost is A$49 per person.

Kakadu National Park

Kakadu National Park is at 110,000 square km the largest
national park in Australia and it also contains some of the
best examples of Aboriginal rock art. The art at
Nourlangie's Anbangbang gallery is well known and
includes work as recent as 1964, added by Nayombolmi,
of the Badmardi clan. It features the mythical characters
of Namarrgon, Namondjok and Barrginj.

To the west, is Nangawulurr Shelter, a refuge used by the
Warramal clan and another Aboriginal gallery. There is
also rock art at the Ubirr site and movie fans may
recognize this as one of the locations in the Crocodile
Dundee film.

A popular route near Ubirr is the Bardedjilidji Walk, but do check in at the Bowali Visitor Centre beforehand, as the staff there will be able to organize guides and advise you, if there is any flooding hazard. More challenging walks include the 3.6km Mirrai Lookout Walk and the 12km Barrk Sandstone Walk, which passes features like Nourlangie Rock and Nanguluwur Art Gallery.

Besides the rock art, you may also see plenty of wildlife, such as wallabies, frilled lizards and even groups of feral pigs, water buffalo and horses. There are fascinating termite mounds, rugged mountains and colonies of wetland birds, like the enigmatic 'Jesus' bird that cruises from lily pad to lily pad, ospreys, sea eagles, magpie geese, egrets and herons. A great place for watching the wildlife is the Yellow Water Billabong, a placid estuary of the East Alligator River.

At the southern end of Kakadu, you can see the dramatic sight of the 200m Jim Jim Falls (http://www.jimjimfalls.com/) and Twin Falls. That is, unless you visit in the dry season between July and October, when it becomes a barren gorge. If you dare, do book a crocodile spotting river cruise. A great place to relax and picnic is the Gunlom Plunge Pool. Whatever you plan to do at Kakadu National Park, do bring lots of bottled water as temperatures can exceed 40 degrees Celsius.

Warradjan Cultural Centre

Kakadu Highway, Jim Jim,
Kakadu National Park,
Northern Territory 0886, Australia
Tel: +61 8 8979 0145
http://www.gagudju-dreaming.com/Indigenous-Experience/Warradjan-Cultural-Centre.aspx

The Warradjan Cultural Centre shares informative material on the region's geography, history and indigenous fauna and flora. Some of the subjects covered include mythology, celestial events and various rites of passage. There is also a gift shop that sells a large selection of Aboriginal art, including bark paintings, as well as books, traditional music and T-shirts. The Warradjan Cultural Centre is air-conditioned and admission is free.

Tiwi Islands

The Tiwi Islands are located about 80km north of Darwin, roughly where the Arafura Sea merges with the Timor Sea. The largest islands are Melville and Bathurst, but there are also nine uninhabited islands. The islands have a combined population of about 3000, of which 90 percent are Aboriginal, but they are believed to have been occupied for around 7000 years. The culture of the islands represent an interesting blend of Aboriginal and Polynesian cultures.

Visitors will need a permit for the islands and there are practically no facilities for tourists. Adventurous visitors may wish to participate in a deep-sea fishing expeditions. Distinctive to the island are elaborately decorated "pukamanis" or burial poles that can be as high as 3m. Most of the carvings depict birds, which are integral to the island's mythology. The Tiwi Islands can be reached by light aircraft from Darwin. There is also a ferry service between Darwin and Bathurst Island. Unique craft items items can be bought on the islands.

Litchfield National Park

http://www.litchfieldnationalpark.com/

Litchfield National Park is located about 100km southwest of Darwin and was named after Frederick Henry Litchfield, one of the first European explorers of the northern end of Australia. The park contains some of the region's best examples of magnetic termite mounds, which can be accessed via a route of boardwalks.

Other features include the Bamboo Creek tin mine, several waterfalls such as Wangi Falls, Tjaynera Falls, Surprise Creek Falls and Florence Falls and Blyth Homestead, which was built in 1929. Some of the indigenous wildlife includes kangaroo, wallaby, possums, flying foxes, dingo and ghost bats, as well as a large variety of bird species such as the black kite, yellow oriole, figbird and rainbow bee-eater. The park is home to isolated sections of monsoon rainforest, but also has lovely ground orchids. There are various camping and caravan sites.

Alice Springs

Alice Springs is located right at the heart of Australia. It is just under 1500km from Darwin to the north and about 1500km from Adelaide to the south. If you want the remoteness of the Outback to hit home, visit two unique facilities created to bridge some of the large distances of the region. Both the School of the Air and the Royal Flying Doctors Service are headquartered in Alice Springs.

The School of the Air is located at 80 Head Street and provides a glimpse into some of the challenges faced by educators in order to bring schooling to students on remote ranches, some as far as 1500km away. Initially a radio service, the School of the Air now utilizes computers and satellite communication. Also based in Alice Springs is the visitors centre of the Royal Flying Doctors Service (http://www.rfdsalicesprings.com.au/).

This life saving service, founded by John Flynn in 1928, operates from 21 bases and promises to be able to reach any patient within the coverage area in two hours. At the Visitors Centre, you can watch an informative video and also see some of the early equipment used. Then, compare that to the modern technology of today, which can track any plane in the service in real time. Finally, take a good look inside a replica of one of the specially adapted planes. Admission is A$12, with an optional A$2 to see the inside of the plane. A gift shop sells branded merchandize.

In Alice Springs, the Great Outdoors is huge, and instantly accessible. Animal lovers will probably enjoy a visit to the Kangaroo Sanctuary (https://www.kangaroosanctuary.com/). Here they can meet kangaroo rescuer, Brolga, featured as Kangaroo Dundee on BBC2 and his charges, which includes the enormous male, Roger. Booking is essential. A sunset tour costs A$85. The Alice Springs Reptile Centre is located opposite the Flying Doctor's Visitors Centre. There are around 30 different species such as bearded dragons, pythons, iguana, blue tongued lizards, gecko, crocodiles and sand goanna and visitors will have the opportunity to handle some of these. Admission is A$13.

Car enthusiasts should consider a visit to the Road Transport Hall of Fame (http://www.roadtransporthall.com/), where they can meet some of the mechanical workhorses of the past. The National Pioneer Women's Hall (http://www.pioneerwomen.com.au/) showcases the achievements of various women who were pioneers of their field. A prize exhibit is a quilt featuring the signatures of most of the women included in the display. The Alice Springs Telegraph Station Reserve once served as an important link in the chain of communication between Adelaide and Darwin. Established in 1873, it was operational for almost six decades and was later utilized as a school for Aboriginal children. It is located along South Stuart Highway.

For a good overview of what Alice Springs has to offer, why not book a ride aboard the hop-on-hop-off town tour (http://www.alicewanderer.com.au/12-alice-explorer-hop-hop-off-town-tour.html), which stops at various of the town's attractions such as the Old Telegraph Station, Anzac Hill, the Royal Flying Doctor Base, Reptile Centre, Olive Pink Botanical Garden and Todd Mall. A ticket costs A$44.

Camel Tours

Camels once played an integral role in creating the infrastructure of Australia's remotest regions. Cameleers from Afghanistan, who arrived down south from the 1860s, were the pioneers of long distance land travel in the Australian outback. For decades, they delivered mail and supplies and when railways and highways were constructed, they provided labour as well as the back-up of transporting vital provisions. Historically, the area was also policed on camelback, a tradition that disappeared in the 1950s.

Today, visitors can explore the region through a camel tour. Camel Tracks (http://www.cameltracks.com/) offers the choice of an hour-long excursion for A$60 or a half day tour for A$110. The experience can also be customized and camel related souvenirs and collectables are available.

Larapinta Trail

A prominent feature of Central Australia is the MacDonnell mountain range. Here, serious hikers would be presented with the challenge of the Larapinta Trail, a 223km route that leads from Alice Springs to Mount Sonder, which is, at 1380m, one of the highest mountains in the West MacDonnell mountain range after Mount Zeil.

The route has a number of fascinating geographical landmarks, including Brinkley's Bluff, Glen Helen Gorge, Counts Point, Standley Chasm, Ellery Creek Waterhole, Serpentine Gorge and Ormiston Gorge and the Ochre Pits a multi-coloured, layered rock used for Aboriginal Ceremonies. Hikers are strongly advised to schedule their trips for the winter months, from June to August, as summer temperatures in the area can reach around 45 degrees Celsius, creating the risk of heatstroke and dehydration.

Alice Springs Desert Park

Larapinta Drive,
Alice Springs,
Northern Territory 0871, Australia
Tel: +61 8 8951 8788
http://www.alicespringsdesertpark.com.au/

The Alice Springs Desert Park introduces visitors to the natural fauna and flora of a desert environment.

Highlights of the park's attractions are the bird show, which displays the skills of its raptors and the guided nocturnal tour. Admission is A$25. The park has a program that offers students the opportunity to volunteer in various fields such as animal keeping and horticulture.

Ayers Rock (Uluru)

http://www.uluru.com/

The enigmatic Ayers Rock, or Uluru, to use its aboriginal name, is a massive sandstone structure located in the middle of the Australian Outback, about 450 km from Alice Springs and what you see, is the just a fraction. The largest part of the rock is subterranean and extends 2.5km below the ground. The Aboriginal people believe that the underground portion of Uluru is hollow and taps into a powerful well of energy and life force, which they refer to as Tjukurpa and also the Dream time. It functions as a connection to the ancestors, as well as some type of Akashic record.

The rock was discovered by the surveyor William Gosse in 1873 and named after Sir Henry Ayers, the Chief Secretary of South Australia at the time. One unique feature is the way the colour of the light changes, as the angle of the sun does, so that the rock appears in different hues at different times of the day. Its orange-red colour is the result of surface oxidation of the iron component of the rock.

The rock formation is believed to contain 25 to 35% quartz. Uluru is 3.6km long and 1.9km wide, rising 348m above the plain, but its true height is 860m above sea level. Some of Uluru's caves feature rock art dating back 5000 years.

Uluru/Ayers Rock was listed twice as a World Heritage site initially in 1987 for its distinctive geographical features and subsequently, in 1997, for its cultural significance to the aboriginal people of Australia. It is regarded as a holy site by the Anangu people, who have lived in the area for approximately 10,000 years. Uluru itself is estimated to be around 600 million years old. It is classified as an inselberg, a term used to describe an "island mountain." Hard to believe now, but this structure began its existence as compressed sediment at the bottom of an ocean.

A trip to Uluru/Ayers Rock can be combined with a cultural experience that will introduce visitors to the indigenous plant and animal life of the region, educate them about bush food and share folk tales and myths about the state of being the Aboriginals refer to as Dream Time. Various types of guided tours are available. Among these options, you can choose from Harley-Davidson tours, Sunrise tours, Sunset tours, stargazing tours, helicopter tours and camel excursions. A 10.6km looped walk around the base of Uluru will impress you with its size and introduce you to its geographical diversity, as well as its indigenous animal and plant life. At the Cultural Centre, you can learn more about the Rock, buy snacks, arts, crafts and souvenirs from the locals and even enjoy a BBQ. A visit to Uluru is often combined with a trip to Kata Tjuta. Uluru is visited by around 250,000 visitors each year.

Kata Tjuta is located within the same National Park as Uluru. Its highest peak, at 1,066m above sea level, is Mount Olga, which was named after Queen Olga of Württemberg. In the 1950s, the area was made into a National Park, disregarding indigenous claims to the land. In the 1980s, the sites were finally restored to the ownership of Anangu people. There is an agreement of joint management between the Anangu and Australian Parks.

Katherine

Katherine, the third largest settlement in the Northern Territory, is located along the banks of the Katherine river. The river also flows through Katherine Gorge, which is in turn one of the most striking features of the Nitmiluk National Park. The park is 30km from Katherine and also features a scenic but challenging bush-walking route, Jatbula trail, which passes impressive waterfalls as well as the Jawoyn Aboriginal rock art site. About 30km from Katherine along the Stuart Highway, you will find the Cutta Cutta Caves, a network of limestone caves with interesting Karst features. Mataranka, a small township 107km from Katherine, has hot springs and is associated with a well known Australian novel, We of the Never Never by Jeannie Gunn. Popular activities of the region around Katherine include bushwalking, canoeing and helicopter tours. Bear in mind that there is a significant flooding risk during the wet season at most of Katherine's attractions.

Katherine Museum

Gorge Rd

One of the more unusual exhibits at Katherine Museum is a planetarium hand made by one of the area's more eccentric residents, a Russian peanut farmer known as Galloping Jack. There are also various collections of historical photographs, ancient Aboriginal artefacts and relics from World War Two. Admission is A$10.

Recommendations for the Budget Traveller

Places to Stay

Paravista Motel

5 Mackillop Street, Parap,
Darwin, Northern Territory 0820, Australia
Tel: +61 8 8981 9200
http://paravistamotel.com.au/

Located in a quiet street in the Parap Village suburb of Darwin. The Paravista motel has a retro 1970s atmosphere and is conveniently near a number of great shopping opportunities.

The motel has a pool and spa, communal kitchen and BBQ area, laundry and tours can be booked through the Tours desk. Free parking is available. Rooms include air-conditioning, a private bathroom, fridge, television, coffee and tea making facilities and free Wi-Fi internet. Accommodation is charged from A$89 during the wet season and A$129 during the dry season. Larger groups may wish to consider renting a three bedroom house at between A$250 and A$325.

Palms Motel

100 McMinn Street,
Darwin, Northern Territory 0800, Australia
Tel: +61 8 8981 4188

Palms Motel is located a short drive from the city centre and a 10 minute walk from the botanical gardens. The motel has an outdoor pool and BBQ facilities. There is also free parking, a DIY laundry service and vending machines. Each room includes en suite bathroom and a kitchenette with microwave, fridge and tea and coffee making facilities. Accommodation begins at A$118. Internet access is not available.

Ashton Lodge

48 Mitchell Street,
Darwin, Northern Territory 0800, Australia

Centrally located in Mitchell Street above the Wisdom
Bar, Ashton Lodge is somewhere between a motel and a
backpackers lodge. There is a swimming pool, terrace,
bar, laundry facilities and a communal kitchen, and
guests also qualify for a 10 percent discount at the
Wisdom Bar. Bear in mind, though, that this vibrant
setting can get a little noisy at night. Rooms are basic, but
clean and well-maintained. Wi-Fi coverage is available,
but charged separately. Accommodation begins at A$110.

Value Inn

50 Mitchell Street,
Darwin, Northern Territory 0801, Australia
Tel: +61 8 8981 4733
http://www.valueinn.com.au/

The Value Inn is centrally located in the lively Mitchell
street. There is a swimming pool with pool bar, a
dedicated BBQ area, a waterfall spa, self-catering kitchen,
laundry facilities and an internet cafe. Reception is
available round the clock. All rooms include en suite
bathroom facilities, TV, a bar fridge and tea and coffee
making facilities. Accommodation begins at A$135.

Dingo Moon Lodge

88 Mitchell Street,
Darwin, Northern Territory 0800, Australia
http://www.dingomoonlodge.com/

Since accommodation in Darwin can be quite pricey, you may seriously consider sacrificing a few creature comforts for the cheaper options at hostels or backpackers accommodation. Mitchell Street is a very good place to start looking for some of those. Dingo Moon Lodge is located a little way off from the main night spots and offers very friendly service. There is also the added bonus of free laundry and a free breakfast. The communal kitchen can get somewhat crowded and rooms are small and basic. Wi-Fi internet coverage is available. Accommodation ranges from dorms for eight, six and four, to double rooms shared between two, with rates from A$24 for the most basic dorm bed to A$102 per room, for two.

Places to Eat & Drink

The Deck Bar Restaurant

22 Mitchell Street,
Darwin, Northern Territory, Australia
Tel: +61 8 8942 3001
http://www.thedeckbar.com.au/

The Deck Bar restaurant combines friendly service and a great atmosphere with meals at reasonable prices. There is indoor and outdoor seating and a selection of around 80 beers and numerous creative cocktails. The menu is varied and includes regular favourites such as pizza, salads, burgers and grills, as well as a large selection of Asian style dishes such as laksa, pad thai and curry.

If you're interested in nibbling and sharing, try one of the platters, priced between A$25 and A$45, which includes different combinations of snacks such as spring rolls, chicken wings, skewers, fries and rice paper rolls. Alternately, tapas style snacks can be ordered and these include lamb cutlets, dumplings, duck pancakes and spicy salt squids. If you love burgers, try the Double Decker for A$19.90, which is served with fries and salads. Dinner mains are priced between A$14.50 and A$29. Breakfast and brunch options are priced between A$9.50 and A$16. The Deck Bar restaurant also features live or DJ entertainment.

Speaker's Corner Cafe Restaurant

Mitchell Street, Parliament House,
Darwin, Northern Territory, Australia
Tel: 08 8946 1439
http://www.karensheldoncatering.com/speakers_corner
_cafe

For a wholesome breakfast to start your day or a light, but filling lunch, take a seat at Speaker's Corner Cafe. Some of the fare will be reminiscent of England. There is a great selection of sausage rolls and pies such as cornish, beef and mushroom, creamy chicken or chunky lamb, all priced at between A$5 and A$8. Fish and Chips will set you back around A$18 and expect to pay A$16 for a Classic Aussie burger with chips. Be sure to check out daily specials such as the roast of the day or the quiche of the day. Speaker's Corner Cafe also serves slices of cake, freshly squeezed juices, smoothies, milkshakes, muesli and toast. The restaurant is open between 7.30am and 4pm.

Sari Rasa Restaurant

6/24 Cavenagh Street,
Darwin, Northern Territory 0800, Australia
Tel: +61 8 8941 9980

Sari Rasa is a small cafe that offers authentic Indonesian cuisine at budget prices.

Some of the favourites include beef redang, chilli beans and eggplant and dried beef with crispy potatoes. There is a good selection of curries, such as beef, chicken, lamb and fish curry. A large portion costs A$12 and includes the choice of three mains and rice.

Kakadu Bakery Restaurant

Gregory Pl, Jabiru,
Kakadu National Park, Northern Territory, Australia
Tel: 8979 2320

At the Kakadu Bakery you can buy a variety of snacks, treats and light meals on your way to or from the National Park. Service is quick and efficient. Some of the choices include freshly prepared salad, quiches, pizza slices, sandwiches, burgers, cakes and pastries. At between A$4.50 and A$5, the pies are a popular choice and some of the fillings include crocodile, kangaroo meat, buffalo and mushroom.

Page 27 Cafe Restaurant

3 Fan Arcade,
Alice Springs, Northern Territory, Australia
Tel: 08 8952 0191

Located at the end of Todd Mall, Page 27 is a 1960s style cafe with great ambiance that serves breakfast and lunch. There are salads, omelettes, cakes, smoothies, muffins and corn fritters, as well as pies and pita wraps. Expect meals between A$8 and A$16.

Places to Shop

Parap Shopping Village

Parap Road, Parap Village Shopping Precinct,
Darwin, Northern Territory 0820, Australia
http://parapvillage.com.au/

There are several shops of interest at Parap Shopping
Village. Nomad Art sells indigenous craft items sourced
from various Aboriginal Art Centres. The Good Luck
Shop (http://www.goodluckshop.com.au/) sells a large
selection of gifts and wellness products, including
incense, wind chimes, essential oils, aromatic candles,
grass woven baskets, jewellery, Egyptian perfume and
other novelty items.

Goods include crafted items from Swaziland, Tibet,
Zimbabwe, India, the Philippines and Vietnam.
Outstation showcases the work of established and
upcoming indigenous artists and items include wall
hangings, paintings, woven handbags and toys. Another
gallery selling the work of Aboriginal artists is the Tiwi
Art Network, which specifically focuses on the work of
artists from the Tiwi Islands. For gifts and novelty items,
check out the wares at Paraphernalia. Parap Village also
has various salons, spas, restaurants and other shops.

Besides regular trade, Parap Village is home to one of Darwin's longest running markets. The market trades every Saturday from 8am to 2pm and features a large selection of arts and crafts, clothing, jewellery, handmade soaps, musical instruments, decor items and skin care products.

Choose from Vietnamese silk scarves, sarongs, pearls and many more. Besides crafts, there is also a great choice in local fresh produce, flowers, herbs and spices and ready made food. You can snack on Nutella crepes, rice paper rolls, papaya salad and various Asian favourites.

Mindil Beach Markets

Darwin,
Northern Territory, Australia
http://www.mindil.com.au/

Enjoy the beach setting, the beautiful sunset and the live entertainment, which ranges from fire breathers and jugglers to didgeridoo players at Mindil Beach Market. The market has around 60 food stalls, which sell juices, smoothies, ice cream, fruit salad, muffins, burgers, hot dogs, kebabs, sushi, pizza, pasta, BBQ seafood and even crocodile fillets. You can choose from Chinese, Thai, Indian, Mexican, Greek and Sri Lankan food.

The other stalls feature a diverse selection, which includes gems, fabrics, collectible coins, art, handmade puzzles, books, didgeridoos, toys, T-shirts and jewellery from around well over 100 local crafters. There is also a wellness section where you can indulge yourself with a Thai massage, a Chinese massage or a foot massage, consult a tarot reader or try some of the local skin care products or natural bush remedies. Do bear in mind that the venue has no facilities for credit card transactions.

Casuarina Square

Trower Road, Darwin
http://www.casuarinasquare.com.au/

The largest shopping mall in the Northern Territory is Casuarina Square, which is located in the northern suburbs of Darwin. Most major stores have outlets here, and there is also a number of speciality shops. There are two supermarkets, Coles and Woolworths, as well as Kmart, Just Jeans and Priceline. Dollars and Sense (http://www.dollarsense.com.au/) stocks a large variety of items including toys, clothing, home ware, gifts and craft items.

Visit Smiggle (http://www.smiggle.com.au/shop/en/smiggle/) for colorful novelty items such as lava lamps, bracelet kits, card making kits, a selection of puzzles and a colour-changing brolly (umbrella). J & V Gifts 'n' Novelty (http://www.jvgiftsnnovelty.com/) stocks plush toys, merchandize related to popular anime and computer games, figurines and other toys.

di CROCO

Shop 4, The Vic Complex
27 The Mall, Darwin NT 0800 Australia
Tel: +61 8 8941 4470
http://www.dicroco.com/

Crocodiles are synonymous with Australia. Therefore it should not come as too much of a surprise that the country has some great outlets for crocodile hide products. Most crocodile farms you visit should have a gift shop that stocks crocodile related products, but for a great range of crocodile hide products, do browse through the wares at di CROCO. You will be able to choose from belts, handbags of various sizes, wallets, purses, pouches, business and travel accessories and also jewellery such as bangles, bracelets, beads, rings, earrings, studs and cufflinks.

Shopping in Alice Springs

At the Todd Mall market, held Sundays from May to December, you can expect plenty of crafts, jewellery and Aboriginal art, as well as an entertaining crew of entertaining buskers. For a great selection of indigenous art, visit Aboriginal Art World (http://www.aboriginalartworld.com.au/), which showcases the work of over 70 artists from South Australia and the desert interior of the Northern territory. Pitjantjatjara is particularly well represented.

Other galleries include Mbantua Gallery
(http://www.mbantua.com.au), Papunya Tula Artists
(http://www.papunyatula.com.au), an Aboriginal
owned enterprise representing 120 artists and Ngurratjuta
Iltja Ntjarra (http://www.ngurart.com.au). Tjanpi Desert
Weavers (http://www.tjanpi.com.au/) is a non-profit
organization selling woven baskets and also grass
sculptures, such as their desert dogs. Looking for a
shopping mall in Alice? Try Yeperenye Shopping Centre
(http://www.yeperenye.com.au/). For a selection of
personalized gifts, go to Alice Springs Creative Gifts &
Awards at 81 Smith Street. Booklovers should check out
Dymocks in Alice Plaza, Red Kangaroo Books at 79 Todd
Mall or, if they don't mind buying second hand,
Bookmark it, at 113 Todd Street.

Printed in Great Britain
by Amazon